MegaMax

Cas Lester

Illustrated by
Karl West

OXFORD

OXFORD
UNIVERSITY PRESS

Great Clarendon Street, Oxford, OX2 6DP,
United Kingdom

Oxford University Press is a department of the University of Oxford.
It furthers the University's objective of excellence in research, scholarship,
and education by publishing worldwide. Oxford is a registered trade mark of
Oxford University Press in the UK and in certain other countries

British Library Cataloguing in Publication Data
Data available

978-0-19-837760-3

1 3 5 7 9 10 8 6 4 2

Paper used in the production of this book is a natural, recyclable product
made from wood grown in sustainable forests. The manufacturing process
conforms to the environmental regulations of the country of origin.

Printed in China by Leo Paper Products Ltd.

Acknowledgements
Inside cover notes written by Becca Heddle
Author's dog photograph by Cas Lester

Contents

Chapter 1
Mega Brilliant
X-10 TurboChair

It was Saturday morning and Huang had stuck a large sign on the outside of his bedroom door: DO NOT DISTURB, GENIUS AT WORK. Inside the bedroom, Huang (the genius himself) was sitting at his desk working on his latest ingenious invention.

He'd already invented *and built*:

- a machine to make his favourite snack (banana and jam sandwiches)
- a remote control to open any door in the flat (including the fridge and his wardrobe)
- an extendable arm for his wheelchair to reach things he couldn't. (Like the button in the lift to get to the sixth floor – which was where he lived.)

Now he was working on an incredibly ambitious project: the X-10 TurboChair. It was going to be the most mega brilliant wheelchair ever made – rocket-powered, with a built-in jelly bean dispenser, a games console, a wrap-around 3D flexi-screen, a fizzy drink cooler and a top speed of *120 miles per hour*!

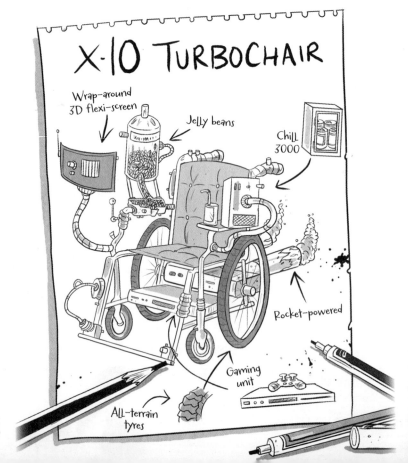

X-10 TURBOCHAIR

Wrap-around
3D flexi-screen

Jelly beans

Chill
3000

Rocket-powered

Gaming
unit

All-terrain
tyres

Frankly, it was amazing that Huang could find any space to work on his desk at all. It was covered with felt tip pens, drawings, old games consoles, screwdrivers, ancient mobile phones and remote controls – including the one for his old toy robot dog. You could barely move for plugs and wires, bits of computers and other electronic gizmos.

Anyhow, this morning he'd shoved everything to one side and was working on the X-10 TurboChair brakes – which were going to have to be mega powerful.

Suddenly, despite the 'Do Not Disturb' sign on the door, Huang's dad popped his head in. He clutched his forehead and gasped dramatically.

"Your room looks like a tornado's hit it!" he cried.

"Really?" said Huang, gazing around the room carelessly.

Huang's bed (which he hadn't made) was strewn with comics, an empty salt and vinegar crisp packet, a dirty plate with half a piece of toast on it, and a soggy brown banana skin. His school uniform and book bag, along with most of his schoolbooks, were scattered across the floor. And for some reason his pyjamas were in the rubbish bin!

"You need to tidy your room!" exclaimed Dad.

"But I'm working on my turbo-charged brakes!" cried Huang.

"You'd better do some *turbo-charged* tidying-up first," replied Dad.

"OK," sighed Huang. Moving back from the desk, he pressed a switch on the arm of his wheelchair.

WHIRR CLUNK!

The extendable grab-arm unfolded and scooped everything up from the floor, while Huang grabbed the stuff on the bed.

Then, using his door remote control, Huang opened his wardrobe. He flung everything inside – including the dirty plate, the half-eaten piece of toast and the soggy brown banana skin!

Feeling pleased with himself, he calmly went back to his desk to work.

But almost immediately his gran, Nai Nai, came in.

"It's your turn to load the dishwasher," she announced.

"Can't I do it later?" asked Huang.

"Sorry, no. We'll need the plates for lunch."

Sighing irritably, Huang went along the hall and into the kitchen, loaded the dishes as quickly as possible and then went back to his room.

"I wish people would stop interrupting me," he moaned, shutting his door.

Less than five minutes later it opened again. It was his grandad, Ye Ye.

"Don't forget to clean out the hamster," said Ye Ye.

"Do I have to do it right now?" groaned Huang. But before Ye Ye could answer, Huang's big sister Bo appeared.

"Have you fed the dog?" she demanded.

"No! It's your turn," said Huang.

"No it isn't."

"Yes it is."

"Isn't."

"Is."

"Isn't."

Ye Ye rolled his eyes and left them to it.

"If you're just going to spend all morning arguing, it'll be quicker to do it myself," said Huang, pushing past his sister. Bo smirked.

"Tidy your room ... load the dishwasher ... clean out the hamster ... feed the dog, *and it's not even my turn*! It's not fair!" muttered Huang crossly. But *finally*, he finished his chores and got back to work.

He'd just picked up the plans again when his mum came in! "Have you done your homework?" she asked.

Huang screamed in frustration. "Aaaaaaaaargh!"

"Whatever's the matter?" cried Mum, reeling backwards.

"How am I *ever* going to build my X-10 TurboChair if I keep having to stop to do my chores and my homework?" Huang pointed at the sign on his door. "Don't you know I'm a Genius at Work?"

"Even a genius has to do his homework," replied Mum.

Huang took a deep breath and tried not to explode. But just then he had an outstandingly Genius Idea ...

Chapter 2
Mega Top Secret

Huang gave up trying to build the X-10 TurboChair (well, for a while). For the next few weeks, he worked on something else after school.

He pinned a new sign on his door.

He worked non-stop and even skipped wheelchair basketball training, missed Pizza and Popcorn Night at the cinema, and didn't go over to his mate Finn's *at all*.

Finally, one Saturday morning he'd finished it. He couldn't wait to show it off, so he took it into the kitchen when everyone was having breakfast.

"What is *that*?" gasped Mum.

"This is MegaMax," announced Huang proudly.

"But what is it?" asked Nai Nai.

"It's a multi-tasking, domestic droid with laser optic eyes and digital voice control," said Huang.

The family exchanged confused looks.

"Yes, but what's one of those?" asked Dad.

Huang sighed. Sometimes it was difficult being the only genius in the house.

"It's a robot," explained Huang.

"Ohhh!" nodded everyone, trying to look wise. Well, everyone except Bo.

"Huh! It looks more like a crash helmet crossed with a rubbish bin to me!" she snorted rudely.

Huang shot her a dirty look.

"So, what does it do?" asked Dad.

"Anything you tell it to," grinned Huang. "Watch!" He turned to the robot and said, "MegaMax, get me a glass of orange juice from the fridge."

"Say 'please'!" corrected his mum.

"You don't say 'please' to robots!" exclaimed Huang.

"You do in this house," replied Mum firmly.

Huang rolled his eyes but said, "MegaMax, I'd like a glass of orange juice, *please.*"

The display panel on the front of MegaMax lit up, a set of lights flickered on and off and then:

BLEEP BEEP

The robot obediently trundled over to the fridge on its caterpillar tracks. It opened the door with one mechanical hand and took out a carton of juice with the other one.

WHIRR CLUNK

Huang's family watched, open-mouthed in surprise. Then a beam of red light shot out from the robot's laser eyes and scanned the label on the carton.

"Is it actually reading?" asked Mum in astonishment.

"Technically, no," replied Huang. "It's just using its laser optic sight to scan the digital information and look it up in the dictionary I downloaded from the Internet."

Huang's entire family turned to stare at him ... slowly. They had no idea what he was talking about. Sometimes it was difficult having a genius in the family.

BZZZZZ SCAN went MegaMax. And then it said "Orange juice" in a funny flat voice.

"It can talk!" gasped Bo.

"Yes," said Huang modestly. "I took the voice control system from Dad's old mobile phone."

MegaMax picked up a glass from the table, poured some juice into it and handed it to Huang.

"A glass of orange juice," it droned.

"Thank you," said Huang, taking it. "MegaMax, please get me a bowl of cereal with milk and sugar."

WHIRR CLUNK CLUNK …
BLIBBLE BLEEP went the robot. Then
to everyone's amazement, it shook some
cereal into a bowl, poured on some milk,
sprinkled sugar on top and handed the
bowl to Huang.

"**Cereal with milk and sugar**," it said.

There was utter silence in the kitchen –
apart from the sound of Huang munching
his breakfast and slurping his orange juice.

Huang's family were speechless. They
knew he was a genius – but he'd never
made anything as remarkable as this before.

"MegaMax is going to do my chores,"
said Huang casually and, between
mouthfuls of cereal, he read MegaMax the
list of his Saturday tasks from the rota on
the fridge.

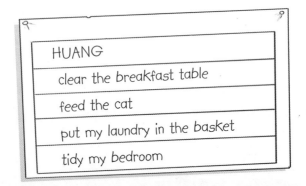

HUANG

clear the breakfast table

feed the cat

put my laundry in the basket

tidy my bedroom

A row of lights on MegaMax lit up as it repeated the list. Then it started picking up the dirty dishes from the table – including Huang's bowl and glass (once he'd finished with them).

"Hey! That's not fair!" exclaimed Bo. "How come Huang gets a robot to do his chores?"

"Because I built one!" grinned Huang over his shoulder as he headed back to his room.

Huang spent the whole of the morning working on the design for the X-10 TurboChair while MegaMax did all his chores.

"I am a genius!" sighed Huang happily.

After lunch, his best mate Finn came over so they could do homework together. They sat at the kitchen table.

"It's literacy," moaned Finn as they opened their books.

Huang rolled his eyes.

There were three short sentences stuck in their books:

The dog barked.
The door slammed.
The cat sat.

"We have to turn them into 'Splendid Sentences' by adding lots of 'Wonderful Words'," groaned Finn. "Bor-ing."

"Hang on!" cried Huang suddenly. "We don't have to do it at all." He grabbed their books and headed off to his bedroom.

"What?" asked Finn, following him.

Huang flung open his bedroom door. "Meet MegaMax!" he cried proudly. "MegaMax, say hello to Finn."

A smiley face emoji appeared on the robot's display screen and it said, "Hello to Finn."

"That's AWESOME!" gasped Finn.

"Yup!" grinned Huang. "This morning it did all my chores, and guess what? Now it's going to do our homework."

"Huang, you're a genius!" Finn laughed.

Huang turned to MegaMax, put up his hand and said, "High five, MegaMax."

MegaMax 'high-fived' Huang with its hard metal hand.

"Ouch!" yelped Huang.

"All we have to do is give the robot a pencil and the books, and tell it what to do," Huang explained to Finn, handing everything over to MegaMax.

"Just add some interesting words to these sentences," he ordered MegaMax.

"Lots of them," added Finn.

"Add lots of interesting words," droned MegaMax obediently.

The boys burst out laughing.

Then they spent the *entire* afternoon playing endless computer games and reading piles of comics while MegaMax bleeped and blipped busily, doing their homework.

It seemed like a good idea at the time.

As it turned out – it wasn't.

Chapter 3
Mega Sticky Problem

On Monday morning Huang excitedly took MegaMax to school for show-and-tell.

MegaMax followed Huang into the classroom, with its caterpillar tracks squeaking across the floor. Everyone fell silent and stared in surprise.

Then,

WHIRR CLATTER CLUNK

MegaMax rolled around the tables and chairs and put Huang's lunch bag on the packed lunch trolley.

Next,

RUMBLE SQUEAK

it trundled over to their teacher, Mrs Bashir.

BLIBBLE BLEEP!

"Here is Huang's homework," droned MegaMax, holding out Huang's book in its mechanical hands.

Mrs Bashir looked at the robot over the top of her glasses and blinked in astonishment.

"Er … thank you," she stammered, taking the book. Then, turning to Huang, she asked, "Where did you get this incredible robot?"

"I built it," grinned Huang. "It can do anything. What would you like it to do?"

"Um ... can it sharpen pencils?" asked Mrs Bashir.

"Easy peasy lemon squeezy!" said Huang.

"Squeezey lemons," repeated MegaMax obediently.

The whole class burst out laughing.

"MegaMax, nooo!" cried Huang. "Not squeezey lemons! Sharpen the pencils!"

"Sharpen the pencils," repeated MegaMax, picking up the class box of pencils from Mrs Bashir's desk. It held the sharpener delicately between its metal fingers. Then,

WHIZZ WHIRR DRRRR!

Its lights flickered briskly as it sharpened all the pencils – in about thirty seconds flat.

When MegaMax had finished, a thumbs-up emoji flashed on to its screen.

"Wow! That was MegaSpeedy!" laughed Mrs Bashir. "Huang, you're a genius. Can you make me a robot too?" she asked.

"Me first!" cried Finn.

"And me?" begged someone else.

"Me too!" yelled the whole class, looking at Huang pleadingly.

Huang was horrified.

"I can't make twenty-nine robots," he cried. "It would take me months."

At playtime Finn and Huang went to play football with some of the others.

"MegaMax is in goal," cried Finn. So the robot rumbled over to the goal mouth.

Everyone lined up eagerly, wanting to beat MegaMax in a penalty shoot-out.

But …

WHIRR … SMACK! WHIRR … PUNCH! WHIRR … CATCH!

The robot didn't let in a single goal.

BLEEP BLIBBLE

A grinning emoji, complete with sunglasses, flashed on and off on its display screen.

"Is MegaMax MegaBrilliant at everything?" grinned Finn.

Huang laughed. "Probably!"

But after break Huang found out he was wrong. Because MegaMax got into a horribly sticky situation.

The school play was going to be *The Rocky Horrible Shipwreck* and Huang's class were making some giant sharks for the set. But this meant cutting out, and then sticking on, hundreds of pointy cardboard teeth.

To be honest, it was very fiddly and everyone was getting fed up doing it, so Huang said, "MegaMax can stick the teeth on."

MegaMax held the squeezy glue bottle in one mechanical hand and the cardboard teeth in the other. Soon it was squirting out glue and sticking on teeth … MegaFast!

WHIRR SQUIRT STICK … WHIRR SQUIRT STICK … WHIRR SQUIRT STICK … it went.

Then, all of a sudden, it started going,

WHIRR SQUIRT BZZZZZ … SCHWEERZ BZZZZZ … TZZZZ TZZZZ … instead.

Its warning lights flashed bright red
… and then a row of sad face emojis
scrolled across its screen.

"Error Error Error," repeated
MegaMax, and then, to Huang's horror,
the robot froze mid-task.

Chapter 4
Mega Trouble!

Feeling worried, Huang rushed to investigate, but the robot had stopped working altogether. Its lights had gone out – as had its display screen.

"Has it run out of power?" asked Finn, coming over.

"I don't think so," replied Huang. "All that buzzing made it sound more like a malfunction in the electrical trip circuit, triggering a shutdown in the power outage."

"Er … what?" asked Finn, totally confused.

Sometimes it was difficult having a genius as a friend.

"I think it's broken down," explained Huang.

"Ah," said Finn. It was pretty clear to Huang what had happened. Dollops of gloopy glue had gummed up the robot's insides.

Mrs Bashir said he and Finn could get MegaMax cleaned up. They took off both of its mechanical hands and cleaned them out thoroughly with paper towels. It took them *ages*. They stayed in at lunchtime to get it done, but finally they managed to sort MegaMax out.

But Huang was beginning to wonder if it had been such a good idea to bring his robot to school.

As it turned out – it wasn't.

Because after lunch, MegaMax got Finn and Huang into an even stickier situation.

As soon as everyone trooped back into class for the afternoon, Mrs Bashir walked over to Finn and Huang.

"I've just looked at your homework books," she announced sternly.

Finn and Huang looked at each other. They'd done their homework – or rather MegaMax had. So what could be the problem?

"Both of you have written exactly the same," said Mrs Bashir.

Huang gasped. He'd forgotten to tell MegaMax to write two lots of different sentences.

"Ooops!" he whispered to Finn.

"Uh-oh!" Finn hissed back.

But it got worse.

"I'm going to read out your 'Splendid Sentences' so that the rest of the class can enjoy them," continued Mrs Bashir, shooting them a look over the top of her glasses.

Finn and Huang exchanged worried glances. They suddenly remembered they hadn't actually bothered to check what MegaMax had written!

Mrs Bashir picked up Huang's book and started reading. "Sentence one," she said. "You've both put: 'The smelly dog barked angrily at the great big fat hairy spaceship.' Sounds more like a splendidly silly sentence to me!"

The class started giggling – except for Huang and Finn. They were horrified!

Mrs Bashir carried on reading. "Sentence two. You've both written: 'The pink fluffy door slammed crossly and completely squashed the cheese and pickle donkey.' Really, boys!"

Finn and Huang groaned while the rest of the class fell about laughing. Even Mrs Bashir was struggling to keep a straight face!

"This one is my favourite!" she joked. "Sentence three. You've put: 'The chocolate cat sat lazily in my bubble bath enjoying a ham and pineapple pizza.' It's all brilliantly creative with lots of wonderful words, but your 'splendid sentences' don't make any sense at all! Honestly you two, anyone would think a robot had done your homework," she finished, looking pointedly at MegaMax.

"Uh-oh!" groaned Finn.

"We are so rumbled," moaned Huang.

Mrs Bashir made them stay in at afternoon break and do some more super sentences, but without MegaMax helping them.

Funnily enough, letting MegaMax 'help' them was the last thing Finn and Huang were going to do.

Chapter 5
More Mega Trouble!

Next Saturday morning at home, Huang confidently set MegaMax off doing his chores. Then he settled happily down at the desk in his bedroom to work on his X-10 TurboChair. He was trying to work out how to link the satnav to the power steering. It was tricky – but he was pretty sure he could do it.

Meanwhile,

BLEEP BLIBBLE BLIP

MegaMax trundled efficiently around the flat doing chores.

WHIRR WHOOSH SPLOSH,

MegaMax watered
the pot plants on
the balcony and
then …
WHIRR
CLATTER
CLATTER

it loaded the
dishwasher and
then …
WHIRR
SHAKE CLUNK

it emptied the
waste bins. And
finally,
SHAKE
RATTLE RATTLE

it fed the dog.

The only problem was these weren't Huang's chores – they were Bo's! Huang's sister had sneakily told MegaMax to do *her* tasks instead. But of course Huang, who was working away in his bedroom, had no idea what she'd done.

Well, not until he went into the kitchen at lunchtime – and found he was in a lot of trouble!

"Huang! You haven't set the table!" cried Dad irritably, trying to dish up.

"Did you forget to feed the cat?"
asked Ye Ye as the poor cat yowled sadly
at his empty bowl.

"Why didn't you put your dirty
clothes in the laundry basket?" exclaimed
Nai Nai, loading the washing machine.

"Huang, have you actually done
any of your chores today?" demanded
Mum crossly.

"I've done all of mine," gloated Bo. "Honestly, Huang, you're so lazy!"

"But I *did* do my chores!" protested Huang. "Well, MegaMax did. I heard him whirring and clunking away so I thought he was doing them …" and then he stopped because Bo was smirking.

It didn't take a genius to work out what she'd done. Huang was furious.

"You got MegaMax to do your chores instead of mine!" he yelled at Bo. "Muu-u-um! Tell her she can't do that."

"Why can't I? It's not fair if I have to do my chores but you don't have to do yours," cried Bo indignantly.

"Yes it is!" snapped Huang.

"No it isn't!" retorted Bo.

"Is."

"Isn't."

"Hey, that's enough from both of you!" said Mum, calming them down.

"Bo does have a point," said Dad.

And, much to Huang's dismay, the rest of the family agreed with him.

"Bo's right. It isn't fair that you have a robot to do all your work when nobody else does," said Mum.

"But it's *my* robot!" said Huang hotly.

"I think everyone should be able to borrow MegaMax," said Nai Nai.

"Noooooo!" cried Huang.

"Yes!" said Nai Nai. "Why should you be the only one who doesn't have to do any work?"

"Because I built it. All by myself – and nobody else did!" exclaimed Huang crossly.

"Well, I think MegaMax should do *everyone's* chores," announced Mum.

"But I made MegaMax to help me – not everybody else. MegaMax is MINE!" shouted Huang, and he stormed off to his bedroom and slammed the door.

While Huang was sulking, Dad took MegaMax to go food shopping with him. MegaMax even put all the food away when they got back.

Then Ye Ye set the robot up to do all the ironing. As soon as it had finished that, Nai Nai got it to wash the car.

And no sooner had MegaMax done that, than Mum wanted it to help her ice a chocolate cake!

Huang sat in his room, reading comics and seething. He was much too angry to even think about the satnav on his X-10 TurboChair.

"It's not fair! I wish I'd never even built MegaMax," he thought miserably.

Then suddenly he heard somebody screaming! It was coming from the kitchen.

"Help!" screamed the voice. "Huang! HELP!"

Chapter 6
MegaMax Meltdown!

Huang rushed to the kitchen, quickly followed by everyone else. It was MegaChaos in there. MegaMax had gone completely crazy!

Waving a wooden spoon around wildly, the robot was deliberately throwing chocolate butter icing all over the kitchen!

"Ice the kitchen," it droned. Its bright red warning lights flashed furiously and it bleeped frantically.

BLIBBLY BLIP BLIBBLY BLIP BLIBBLY BLIP

A single word scrolled repeatedly across its display screen:

MegaMeltdown ... MegaMeltdown ... MegaMeltdown ...

Then suddenly its crash-helmet head started to spin furiously. It began blundering backwards and forwards across the kitchen floor, still hurling icing everywhere!

"Help!" wailed Mum.

"Mum! Are you all right?" cried Huang.

"Mum? Where are you?" yelled Bo.

Mum had taken shelter under the table – which was just as well.

SPLAT!

A dollop of icing splattered against the table leg, only just missing her.

"Huang! Make it stop!" she cried.

SPLAT

WHEEEEE … SPLODGE!

Another large blob of icing whizzed past Huang's shoulder and plastered on to the wall.

GLOOP THWACK

Another lump walloped into Dad's face.

"Take cover!" yelled Dad and he and Bo dived under the table to join Mum. Nai Nai and Ye Ye grabbed the ironing board and used it as a shield. Huang yanked open the fridge door and dashed behind it, hardly daring to peer out. Then, to everyone's complete horror …

CRASH SMASH

MegaMax started unloading the dishwasher – by hurling everything into the rubbish bin!

"**Throw out the dishes**," it said.

"Do something, Huang!" yelled Nai Nai.

"Before it breaks everything!" begged Ye Ye.

But before Huang had a chance to do anything at all …

THUMP CLATTER CLATTER

The robot started emptying all the packets and tins out of the food cupboard – and into the washing machine!

"**Empty the food**," it said.

Then without any warning, MegaMax picked up the cat – and dipped him into the sink, which was full of soapy water!

"YEOOOOWL!" went the cat.

"**Wash the cat**," said MegaMax.

"Huang, make it stop!" cried Bo.

"MegaMax, stop," ordered Huang. "STOP!"

But the robot ignored him.

Fortunately MegaMax soon finished washing the cat and let him go. He shot off looking like a drowned rat.

But *unfortunately* the robot was now trundling over to the hamster cage. Gently, it lifted up the hamster with one mechanical hand. It had a fluffy feather duster in the other one.

"**Dust the hamster**," it droned.

"SQUEAK SQUEAK!" went the hamster.

SQUEAK
SQUEAK

"STOP! MEGAMAX, STOP!" yelled
Huang again – louder this time. But the
robot still didn't seem to hear. It just
put the hamster back in the cage and
then grabbed the vacuum cleaner and
switched it on – and pointed it at the
laundry basket.

Bo's school skirt, Huang's superhero
pyjamas and two of Dad's socks were
instantly sucked up …

"**Vacuum the washing**," said MegaMax.

"What's happened to it, Huang?"
asked Mum.

"It's gone mad!" wailed Bo.

"I think it's gone into overload," said
Huang, from behind the fridge door.

"You've got to do something, Huang!"
yelled Dad.

"Why me?"

"Because it's your robot!" replied
everyone at once.

"But it's not my fault, it's yours!
You've all given it too many jobs to do!"
cried Huang angrily.

"Nonsense! I only told it to tidy the kitchen and vacuum the hall," said Mum.

"And I only set it to sweep the floor and load the washing machine," cried Nai Nai.

"Well I only asked it to empty the cat litter and polish the bathroom mirror," exclaimed Ye Ye.

"And I only said it should empty the dishwasher and throw out the rubbish," snapped Dad.

"I only wanted it to clean out the hamster's cage and make my bed," huffed Bo.

But by now MegaMax was charging around the kitchen following the dog with the broom.

WHIRR WHIZZ SWEEP

The dog thought it was a great game.

"GRRR! WOOF, WOOF!" she went, savaging the brush.

"**Sweep the dog**," droned the robot, its lights flashing furiously.

"Huang! You've got to stop it!" cried
Nai Nai.

"Yes – turn it off!" said Mum.

"I can't!" wailed Huang.

"Why not?" said Nai Nai.

"It doesn't have an OFF switch,"
groaned Huang.

"What?" cried Dad.

MegaMax had gone into MegaMeltdown
and Huang had no idea how to stop it!

Chapter 7
Mega Genius Solution

"What do you mean MegaMax doesn't have an OFF switch?" cried Nai Nai.

"Oh for crying out loud!" said Dad.

"Let me get this straight," said Nai Nai, shaking her head. "You built a powerful robot – without an OFF switch?"

"What sort of genius builds a robot without an OFF switch?" demanded Mum.

"Good question!" agreed Bo.

"Stop going on at me!" cried Huang. "And give me a chance to think."

MegaMax was still following the dog around and around the kitchen with the broom.

WHIRR WHIZZ WHIRR

"Sweep the dog. Sweep the dog," droned the robot repeatedly.

"GRRRR WOOF WOOF," went the dog, biting the broom happily and wagging her tail.

It was the sort of game that could keep them both busy for ages.

Which gave Huang the chance to think.

Hurriedly, he looked around for inspiration. Unfortunately he was trapped behind the fridge door, so his choices were a bit limited. But *fortunately* there was something in the fridge door that gave him an ingeniously Genius Idea.

Well two things actually, a squirty bottle of hoisin and spring onion sauce, and another one of tomato ketchup. And both of them were nearly full.

Huang grabbed one bottle in each hand and flipped open the lids. Then he peered around from behind the fridge, pointed the bottles straight at MegaMax and let rip ...

SQUIIIIIRT WHOOOSH
Dollops of sticky hoisin and
spring onion sauce splattered all over
MegaMax, quickly followed
– SQUIRT SPLATTER –
by a generous coating of ketchup!

It didn't take long for the super sticky sauces to seep into MegaMax's works and gum them up completely – just like the glue had done in class!

And so soon, to Huang's relief, MegaMax started going,

WHIRR BZZZZZ SCHWEERZ BZZZZZ TZZZZ TZZZZ

(Just like it had in class!)

And its bright red warning lights flashed urgently … and a row of sad face emojis scrolled across its screen.

"Error Error Error," droned MegaMax. (Again, just like it had in class!)

TZZZZ

SCHWEERZ

BZZZZZ

And then the robot froze in mid-action … and stopped working altogether. (Um, again, just like it had in class!)

"Woohoo!" yelled Huang triumphantly.

The dog was hugely disappointed – but everyone else cheered.

"Huang! You're a genius!" cried Mum, clambering out from under the table and giving Huang a huge hug.

It took the rest of the day to clear up the chaos in the kitchen, but everyone helped. Even the dog (mostly by licking up all the mess).

The next morning Mum called a family meeting to decide What To Do About MegaMax.

"Can you mend it?" she asked Huang.

"Yes. But I'm not going to."

"But it's useful having a robot to do the housework," pleaded Dad.

"Especially the boring things," said Ye Ye.

"And the dirty things," agreed Nai Nai.

"And the difficult things," nodded Mum.

"And the smelly things," said Bo.

"But that's just it. MegaMax can't do *everything*," cried Huang. "You'll just overload it and break it again. And it's not even yours!"

Huang's family exchanged embarrassed, guilty looks. And then they all said sorry to Huang.

"You're right," nodded Mum. "Just because you have a robot that *can* do everything doesn't necessarily mean it *should* do everything."

"Maybe MegaMax could just do *some* of the chores," suggested Dad.

At which point, of course, Huang had one of his Genius Ideas.

"Let's give MegaMax a list of chores to do like everyone else," he said.

"Huang! You're a genius!" said Bo.

So Nai Nai wrote a new rota for the fridge, with a special column for MegaMax.

That afternoon Huang cleaned and repaired MegaMax, and made one vital change to the robot's design. He fitted a large OFF switch!

And then Huang had another spectacularly Genius Idea.

He put a new sign on his bedroom door. It read:

DO NOT DISTURB
GENIUS AND
ROBOT
AT WORK

Huang got MegaMax to help him build his next invention: the rocket-powered, mega brilliant X-10 TurboChair complete with Internet, satnav, turbo-charged brakes, and a built-in jelly beans dispenser, a games console, a wrap-around 3D flexi-screen, a fizzy drink cooler and a top speed of 120 miles per hour!

About the author

No, that's not me! It's my dog, Bramble!
This is what she usually looks like after a
long walk – soggy, filthy and covered in
muck. We both love walks, but *she* hates
baths and *I* hate bathing her. So I'd like
a robot that could clean her up instead!